ROOTS IN WATER

Richard Nelson

357 W 20th St., NY NY 10011
212 627-1055

ROOTS IN WATER
© Copyright 1991 by Richard Nelson

Written permission is required for live performance of any sort. This includes readings, cuttings, scenes, and excerpts. For amateur and stock performances, please contact Broadway Play Publishing Inc. For all other rights contact: Peter Franklin, William Morris Agency Inc., 1350 6th Ave., NY NY 10019, 212 903-1550.

First printing: November 1991
ISBN: 0-88145-093-6

Book design: Marie Donovan
Word processing: WordMarc Composer Plus
Typographic controls: Xerox Ventura Publisher 2.0 P.E.
Typeface: Palatino
Printed on recycled acid-free paper and bound in the USA.

BY RICHARD NELSON
PUBLISHED BY
BROADWAY PLAY PUBLISHING INC

Plays

AN AMERICAN COMEDY (Mark Taper Forum)
BAL (In the anthology ANTI-NATURALISM;
  Goodman Theater)
BETWEEN EAST AND WEST (Hampstead Theatre
  Club, Yale Rep)
JUNGLE COUP (In the anthology PLAYS FROM
  PLAYWRIGHTS HORIZONS)
RIP VAN WINKLE OR "THE WORKS" (Yale Rep)

Adaptations

DON JUAN by Molière (Arena Stage)
IL CAMPIELLO by Carlo Goldoni (The Acting
  Company)
THE MARRIAGE OF FIGARO by Beaumarchais
  (Guthrie Theater and Broadway)
THREE SISTERS by Chekhov (Guthrie Theater)

ABOUT THE AUTHOR

Richard Nelson's other plays include TWO SHAKESPEAREAN ACTORS (Royal Shakespeare Company), SENSIBILITY AND SENSE (American Playhouse Television), THE END OF A SENTENCE (American Playhouse), PRINCIPIA SCRIPTORIAE (Manhattan Theater Club and the Royal Shakespeare Company), THE RETURN OF PINOCCHIO, THE VIENNA NOTES, CONJURING AN EVENT, and THE KILLING OF YABLONSKI.

His other translations and adaptations include Brecht's JUNGLE OF CITIES and THE WEDDING (BAM Theater Company), Erdman's THE SUICIDE (Arena Stage and The Goodman Theater), and Fo's ACCIDENTAL DEATH OF AN ANARCHIST (Broadway). He also is the author of the book for the Broadway musical CHESS, and numerous radio plays for the BBC.

Nelson has received a London TIME OUT Theatre Award, two Giles Cooper Awards, two Obies, a Guggenheim Fellowship, two Rockefeller Playwriting Grants, two National Endowment for the Arts Playwriting Fellowships, and a Lila Wallace *Reader's Digest* Fund Writer's Award.

ORIGINAL PRODUCTION

An earlier version of ROOTS IN WATER was first performed on 23 August 1988 at The River Arts Repertory, Woodstock NY (Lawrence Sacharow, Artistic Director), with the following cast and creative contributors:

Cast: ....Daniel Jenkins
Dan Butler
Deirdre O'Connell
Joanne Camp

Director ....Lawrence Sacharow
Set Designer .... Loy Arcenas
Costume Designer ....Marianne Powell-Parker
Lighting Designer .... Arden Fingerhut
Composer .... Peter Gordon
Stage Manager ....Renee Lutz

This version of ROOTS IN WATER was first presented on the BBC Radio 3 on 2 May 1989 with the following cast and creative contributors:

BUSTER/JACK/FRANK	Alfred Molina
THAI WOMAN/BARBARA/JUDITH	Mary Cornford
JULES JOHNSTONE/JIM	Peter Craze
VERNE/TOM	Sean Baker
ELLEN/MARY	Emily Richard
ROBERT/GEORGE/BILL	Edward Herrman
PETER/GEORGE/BOB	Kerry Shale
LAURA/CHERYL/WILLA	Jane Bertish
DIANE/PHYLLIS/ALICE	Judy Kuhn
JUNE/LYNN	Zoe Wanamaker
APRIL/LIBBY	Shelley Thompson
PETE/FRED	Michael James-Reed
Director	Ned Chaillet
Production Assistant	Maria Evans
Studio Managers	Peter Novis
	Ros Mason
	Jessica Bowles

for Susan Cumings

NOTES

The play is composed of 12, thematically related scenes. No single character appears in more than one of them. Therefore, it is possible to perform the play with two males and two females (if FRED is an off-stage voice in THANKSGIVING) or by three males and two females.

Each scene has a date and a title. These should be projected through the given scene.

The Scenes:

1976, FLYER
1977, BRIEFING
1978, SQUASH
1979, WHAT I DID ON MY SUMMER VACATION
1980, THE ENVIRONMENT
1981, THE FREEZE MOVEMENT
1982, CIVIL RIGHTS
1983, BUYING A HOUSE
1984, THE LAST CIGARETTE or THEY HAVE
   PROBLEMS IN CENTRAL AMERICA
1984, U.S.A. U.S.A. U.S.A.
1986, "THE CHERRY ORCHARD"
1988, THANKSGIVING

There should be an intermission between CIVIL RIGHTS and BUYING A HOUSE.

1.

Projection:

1976
FLYER

(BUSTER, *twenties, sits on a small wooden stool, dressed only in his underwear and a baseball cap. He talks toward the audience, to a woman who is not seen.*)

BUSTER: Now this, what I'm doin', this ain't Nam. I ain't sayin' it is. That was that. And this is this. Now I ain't sayin' that was bad, though 'course I weren't in favor of Nam. Nobody is no more. I'm just sayin' that was tanks and stuff and this, well, it's food and shit. And the only gun I transport now is the one I keep on my hip and that's more a souvenir or something like to do with my hands. So this is real different, okay? *(Beat)* You ever been up in one of them big boys? It's like flying a fuckin' boat, really. Or a whale. Or a tuna. Yeh, it's like sittin' in the eye of some big fat tuna. Like I got these big ol' ropes around the head of this tuna and I'm tellin' it where the fuck to go. I'm flying it, see. I'm the flyer. Fourteen trips so far and I don't think I've slept more than a wink or two in all that time. 'Bout three weeks, I guess. But that's okay, 'cause I know what I'm doing, my mission, see, it's gotta be done. The food, you understand. I bring the food. *(Beat)* God, it's pretty up there. With the tuna. Passing through black clouds. That's clouds that the smoke has reached and that's like death. Like you was moving through closets. And then through the white clouds and that's Heaven, really. Heaven in the sky. And leaning to get a good look at the green hills down there, the thickness that's sort of gone wild, sort of like it's calling up to me, Buster, that a-boy, Buster, you bring us some of that rice 'cause we ain't growing shit but green down here. Shit. *(Beat)* Sometimes I just let Billy, he's my C.O., let him take the reins, let him turn that tuna for a while and I go back into the belly—the part that's pressurized—and I see those crates. Eight ton of crates and I dig my fingers into one and feel the grain like it was gold or something and I'm the king who's got all the gold and that's nice. I like that. *(Beat)* So then as we're coming into the strip, and I see the lights and they hear me coming and sees my eyes lit up, if it's night and not raining or what, and down there I'm watching all them groups of folks and I know as soon as my rubber feet hit that earth they are gonna be off and running after me, and they are gonna be being kicked back like they was asses or something, starving asses, like they've been lost in the desert for a year, 'cause they're so thin, see, and there's so many of them. But I don't look no more, that's at their faces, I mean. I don't look. I mean what's the point in looking, I've looked at too many faces already looking for her. *(Beat)* When I was still looking for her. Which I guess I still am. *(Beat)* But anyway, you can't let yourself be touched, can you. Gotta be like thin steel if you're bringing home the bacon like I am doing. So I don't look, just taxi that big mother tuna to where the guys with the white sticks can keep the ones who don't got no faces away. Gotta be steel. Or you are gonna die, I says. *(Beat)* My sister, she thinks I'm some throwback ape 'cause I think like this. Well if I'm a macho bastard, so what? She's got a briefcase, but she ain't never been faceless. So what the fuck does she know, I says. Fuck her, I says. Fuck. *(Beat)* You sort of look like her. *(Beat)* Not like my sister, I mean. I mean her. Like my wife. *(Beat)* I'd ask you if you know her, but I asked that everywhere already and if I ask it one more time I think I won't be steel no more. Okay? *(Beat)* How'd a gal like you, you know. This business ain't for a pretty gal like you. But gotta eat, right? That's it, right? But shit, I don't like it. Especially 'cause you sort of look like her. Liu Sung. I wish I knew where she was. *(Beat)* But shit, you know. Shit. *(Beat)* Eight tons, sometimes ten tons in a tuna that ain't supposed to carry six tons, but I'm flying it, see. So that's my worry. So I'm in a hurry, you know I gotta feed 'em. That's what I say to mister clip-board. He says—six ton limit, Buster, and I say, sure; the rest, I tell him, the other four tons, well that's my carry-on-luggage. So fuck off. I gotta feed a nation, 'cause she's my wife and if I can't find her in this mess then damn it I'll feed a whole god-forsaken country 'cause if I've fed that country then I know I've fed her and that's my job, ain't it, 'cause she's my wife, damn it. She's gonna eat my rice, that I bring. So go to hell. *(Beat)* It's my only way to be a husband. Hell. *(Beat)* So Buster is steel. And I'm gonna cut through the night like I was a knife, you know, cut through the night with my eyes, my tuna eyes ablaze and bring home the bacon. It's something. *(Beat)* I'm gonna feed a whole son of a bitch continent. *(Beat)* It's something. *(Beat)* It's something. *(Pause)* You gonna suck me off now?

BLACKOUT

2.

Projection:

1977
BRIEFING

(Office. Bangkok. Wooden table, chair, overhead fan, potted palm, three-drawer file cabinet. Telephone.)

(Congressman JULES JOHNSTONE *stands leaning against the filing cabinet, looking out the "window".* BEN VERNE, *his speechwriter, is at the typewriter.)*

(Pause)

*(*VERNE *types.)*

JOHNSTONE: Hot. *(*VERNE *types. Short pause.)* Hot.

VERNE: *(Typing)* Huh?

JOHNSTONE: Hot. The heat.

VERNE: Oh yeh. *(Types)* Couple of minutes more; it's coming. *(Types)* How much time?

JOHNSTONE: Quarter of an hour. *(*VERNE *nods, types. Pause.)* Not hot like Buffalo hot though.... More like D.C. hot, wouldn't you say? *(Short pause)* Or maybe Mobile hot. Ever suffered through Mobile heat? Now that is hot. Christ. That's hot. Like this.

VERNE: *(Typing)* Like this.

JOHNSTONE: Yeh. *(Pause.* VERNE *types.)* Beautiful country though. This. Beautiful part of the world. Too bad about everything.... But still beautiful. Green hills. Mists.... Not really green, almost a blue, don't you think? ...At least in the mist. In the morning. *(Pause.* VERNE *stops typing, thinks.)* Like West Virginia, in a way. *(*VERNE *types.)* Sort of like West Virginia. Thick forests. Great camping. Nobody knows about West Virginia, you know. Big secret, West Virginia.

God, what camping. Beautiful.... Except for the pagodas, like this.

VERNE: *(Typing)* And the heat.

JOHNSTONE: And the heat, right. But still, too bad about everything. Makes you sick.

VERNE: What does?

JOHNSTONE: Everything. *(Beat)* Except the beauty. Makes you think, doesn't it? Makes you ask yourself, how the hell, you know? *(VERNE types.)* It's snowing in Buffalo.

VERNE: *(Typing)* No.

JOHNSTONE: Or was.

VERNE: *(Typing)* Oh yeh?

JOHNSTONE: Two days ago. Read it in the *Tribune*. Eight inches in Buffalo. What a mess, I'll bet. I mean, it isn't even Thanksgiving.

VERNE: *(Typing)* Almost.

(Pause. VERNE types.)

JOHNSTONE: Won't last.

VERNE: Who's going to stop it?

JOHNSTONE: The snow, I mean. Ground's not frozen yet. Just slush in a day. Just slush by now. What a mess, you know. *(Beat)* You got snow tires?

VERNE: *(Typing)* What? No.

JOHNSTONE: Me neither. First snow always catches me. Eight inches. Brother, it's hard to imagine. *(Beat)* Ben?

VERNE: *(Typing)* I'm here.

JOHNSTONE: What do you think about pajamas?

VERNE: *(Typing)* I'll be done in a minute.

(VERNE types. Short pause.)

JOHNSTONE: I'd been wondering what to get Barbara. Then it dawned on me last night. Thailand—the

orient—silk pajamas. Sort of appropriate, don't you
think? *(Beat)* Can't for the life of me think what else to
get her. *(Pause.* VERNE *types.* JOHNSTONE *looks back out
the "windows".)* No. It's not like upstate. Upstate's
different from this. Upstate's more like Northern
Michigan. This is more like West Virginia. Or, say,
Tennessee.

*(*VERNE *suddenly pulls the paper from his typewriter.)*

VERNE: Finished.

*(*JOHNSTONE *walks slowly to* VERNE, *takes the paper,
clears his voice, and begins to read, as if to an audience.*
VERNE *smokes and listens.)*

JOHNSTONE: "Gentlemen, I would like to read a brief
statement. After which I will take your questions.
(Beat) "For the past three days and two nights I have
been visiting refugee camps along the Thai border.
Let me say first, as a human being, and only second as
a United States Congressman, how hard and painful
it has been to maintain one's calm in the face of such
tragedy...." *(Beat)* "Amotionally"?????

VERNE *(Looks at the paper)* Sorry. Typo, should be an
"e".

JOHNSTONE: *(Continuing)* I thought you'd made up
a word. "Emotionally, my visits have been almost
overwhelming. Man's inhumanity to man, I fear,
has rarely been so starkly displayed. The sheer
awesomeness of the numbers jogs the mind: five
million homeless, three million butchered, and twice
that number now starving, dehydrated and bloated,
so weak that they cannot open their eyes. Disease
appears to be the norm here; and medicine the
exception. But numbers aside, it is the people
that one is moved by, those I have talked to, touched,
and watched, feeling more helpless than I have ever
felt before. There is a disgrace happening here, a
disgrace happening here...."

(JOHNSTONE *looks up.*)

VERNE: Yes. I thought you could say it twice.

JOHNSTONE: *(Continuing)* "...a disgrace on all mankind. This is genocide and simple...."

VERNE: *(Looks at the paper)* "Pure and simple." I left out a word.

JOHNSTONE: "Pure and simple." *(Continues)* "And we are witnesses to a race being systematically extinguished. As an American—and, I might add, as one who fought long and hard against our involvement in Southeast Asia—I am doubly pained, for as Americans I think we should bear some of the guilt for these horrendous events, and learn to accept some of the responsibility for helping this ravaged land. And with this in mind I pledge on my return to Washington and to my Buffalo constituency to do all I humanly can to mobilize our government and our people toward the effort of alleviating the sad and terrible situation as it exists here. Thank you. Now I will take questions." *(Nods)* That's fine, Ben. Good job. *(Phone rings.)*

VERNE: *(Into the phone)* Hello? Yes. I'm sorry, can you speak up? Just a minute please. *(To JOHNSTONE)* It's my wife. My call's finally gone through.

JOHNSTONE: Then I'll see you in the briefing room in about five minutes? *(JOHNSTONE exits with the speech.)*

VERNE: Hello, Julie?! God, it's good to hear your.... What? Oh, you know, it's.... *(Beat)* How are the...? It's, you know. I'll tell you about it when I.... Yeh, I guess it's pretty bad. I mean, I don't guess, I sort of know it is. How are...? Yes, I've seen it. You know, we went to some camps somewhere. Imagine the worst then double that. *(Beat)* How...? Well, it's like the whole country is.... Well it's like, uh.... Well, they're dying. Yeh. I mean, they are dying, it's not "like" they're dying. Uh, uh. I mean, they're not all dead yet, but they're about to be, you know. They're sort of sitting there and uh. *(Beat)* Uh. *(Beat)* I said, they're sitting there and about to.... *(Beat)* Uh. *(Beat)* What? No, I'm fine. It's just that. Well, I'm sort of.... I mean, it's sort of hard. I don't think I can really.... Put words to.... Really describe what.... I can't describe what this is.... I mean, this.... *(Beat)* And how you'd even begin to...I...uh.... *(Beat)* Uh. *(Beat)* Hey, how are the kids?

BLACKOUT

3.

Projection:

1978
SQUASH

(Night. Suburban kitchen.)

(Sink. Dishwasher. Counter. After a small party.)

(ROBERT washes plates and glasses. He has a drink to his side.)

(Pause)

(ELLEN enters. Both around thirty.)

ELLEN: He's still asleep.

ROBERT: Uh-huh.

ELLEN: It's the bear tonight.

ROBERT: Huh.

ELLEN: That's three nights in a row for the bear. Maybe he's given up the blanket for good. *(Beat)* For the bear.

ROBERT: Maybe.

(Short pause)

ELLEN: Thinking?

ROBERT: What?

ELLEN: You want to think?

ROBERT: No no.

(Short pause)

ELLEN: Amazing isn't it?

ROBERT: What, the bear? I had a bear.

ELLEN: Not that. I'm getting to think he can sleep through almost anything.

ROBERT: Why?

ELLEN: The noise. It has been pretty noisy.

ROBERT: Has it? Hadn't noticed. *(Reaches for his drink)* Sip?

ELLEN: *(Shakes her head)* Thanks. *(Short pause)* Is that full?

ROBERT: What is?

ELLEN: Is the machine full? Is that why you're washing?

ROBERT: Oh. I forgot. Just started washing.

ELLEN: Here, let me.

ROBERT: No no.

ELLEN: Please. It'll give me something to do. I shouldn't have had that coffee.

(Short pause)

ROBERT: Then I'll dry.

ELLEN: The machine dries.

ROBERT: Oh. Sure. *(Pause)* Was *I* loud? Is that what you meant? That I was loud.

ELLEN: No. You know—politics. Peter was even louder.

ROBERT: But I was still "loud"? Was I obnoxiously loud or just sort of normal everyday loud?

ELLEN: We all talked. We have talky friends. Anyway, he didn't wake up, so who cares?

ROBERT: Thanks to the blanket.

ELLEN: The bear.

ROBERT: Right. *(Short pause)* It's just that I thought the question was worth raising, that's all. I believe it's an important question. I didn't scream in anyone's ear, did I?

ELLEN: No.

ROBERT: Good. It's a fucking important issue.

ELLEN: I know. I heard.

ROBERT: Sometimes we act like we are so goddamn pure. Well, we're not, that's all I wanted to get across. We are not.

ELLEN: You got that across.

ROBERT: I did. I think I did. Whether he heard me or not is something else again.

ELLEN: He'd have to be deaf.

ROBERT: You know what I mean.

ELLEN: I know what you mean. *(Beat)* You were very articulate, I thought.

ROBERT: Yes? *(She nods.)* It's not easy. It is not an easy thing to face. I mean we were right, too. I'm not dumping on all of it. We were right on the one hand and we were wrong or *maybe* we were wrong on the other hand. It's complicated. That's what I tried to get across. That it's complicated. *(Short pause)* Christ. He's stubborn. He thinks he thinks, but I don't think he really does.

ELLEN: Peter?

ROBERT: I mean I marched too. You'd think he ended the whole goddamn war himself, wouldn't you? Well I'd match my credentials with his anyday. I marched. I got maced. Twice. I was in D.C., was he?

ELLEN: So was I.

ROBERT: What? Oh right. Sure, we both were. Our whole generation was. It was a whole generation thing. The war was wrong, we knew it, and we did something about it. All of us. So when I question Peter, I'm also questioning myself. I don't think he understood that. I don't think he understands that kind of discussion.

ELLEN: *(Shushing him)* Robert.

ROBERT: Yeh, sorry. Thank God for the blanket. *(Beat)* There were two ideas—propositions—that we disclaimed. That we, our whole generation disclaimed. One was that if we let Vietnam fall then Christ, the next thing we'd know there goes Indonesia, goodbye Australia, and here come the red flags along Waikiki Beach. That was one idea. But we disclaimed that. I remember a teacher of mine, my religion professor, telling me that Vietnam and China had been enemies for two thousand years or so, and that their alliance, it was not more than a wink of the eye for them, and even if we do pull out our troops, those two fuckers aren't going to stay pals for more than two minutes. Well, he was right. We were. They went to war, didn't they? They fucking went to war. So fuck the Domino Theory, we were right. Our whole generation was. So I'm proud of that. I am. And I think we all should be. *(Drinks)*

ELLEN: If you really wanted to do something, you could dry out the icebucket.

ROBERT *(Nods, continues)* But that's only one side and just as I tried to tell Peter, I told him, we can't have it both ways, fella. We may want that, we may want to sit on our fat asses and pat ourselves on the back, but shit, if we're going to take the credit, which we deserve— which we certainly deserve—then how about taking a little of the blame too. How about that. At least let's talk about it. I mean —Christ, number

two, the other thing we disclaimed, we all did.
Our whole generation did, we said—no bloodbath.
Impossible. We said those folks want to be left in
peace so if they want communism then that's their
choice. That's up to them. Let them be happy. This
country fucked them up so let's fucking pull out now
and they are going to be happy. We said that. And we
said, let's get out of there fast. No bloodbath. Maybe
some reprisals, but what the hell, they're only human,
but no bloodbath. No bloodbath, Ellen.

ELLEN: I'm listening.

ROBERT: But we were wrong, weren't we? There was.
There is.

ELLEN: Yes.

ROBERT: Look at Cambodia. God. Just look at that.
I'd like Peter to look at that.

ELLEN: Yes.

ROBERT: It makes me sick. It really just makes me sick,
'cause I said—no bloodbath. *(Drinks)* So maybe we
ought to take some of that blame, that's all I'm saying.
So let's talk about it. So maybe we were wrong.
Maybe if we weren't shouting—get out, get out
now—maybe there were other ways. I don't know.
Maybe not. But maybe. *(Beat)* Maybe we made a
judgment and maybe that judgment is now killing
millions of people, they're being butchered over there.
Maybe we—our generation—is not so pure and lily
white as we think. Maybe we got a big bright red
stain on us now and maybe we should *deal* with that,
maybe we should start to *talk* about the guilt of our
generation just as we talked about the guilt of our
fathers', and maybe we'll realize that it's not 'cause
they were so stupid, our fathers, I mean, because they
probably thought they were pure too for a while, after
fighting Hitler and the Marshall Plan and all that.
Maybe. That's all I wanted that stubborn bugger to be

convinced of. *(Beat)* But it was like he wouldn't give in. Like he was too goddamn proud to give in. Shit. *(Pause. Drinks.)* He's so stubborn. And stupid. He probably thinks I just wanted to win an argument because....

(Short pause)

ELLEN: Because?

ROBERT: Squash.

ELLEN: Squash? *(He nods.)* What does squash have to do with winning an argument?

ROBERT: This morning he beat me at squash.

ELLEN: He did?

(Beat)

ROBERT: I got a blister.

ELLEN: Oh. *(Long pause)* You were very convincing, I thought. Very articulate. Far more articulate than Peter.

ROBERT: Yes?

ELLEN: I thought so.

ROBERT: Yes? *(She nods.)* Good. That makes me feel better.

BLACKOUT

4.

Projection:

1979

WHAT I DID ON MY SUMMER VACATION

(A youth hostel in Europe. The canteen. Summer. Wooden table. Three chairs.)

(PETER, an American in his thirties, sits at the table. He is unshaven, his clothes unwashed and wrinkled—the

appearance that he has been living in them for quite some time. He wears a leather jacket, hiking boots. He talks to two young American girls, DIANE *and* LAURA, *both in their early twenties.)*

PETER: It's all changed. Look at it, Christ, will you just look at it. *(He shakes his head.)*

LAURA: Look at what?

PETER: If you have to ask.... *(Beat)* Forget it. I don't know why I come here anymore.

*(*LAURA *and* DIANE *look at each other.)*

DIANE: It used to be different?

PETER: Different? *(He laughs.)* Yes. I guess you could say that. I guess you could call this different.

DIANE: Why is that funny?

*(*PETER *shakes his head.)*

LAURA: Well—so what's different? They redecorate or something?

PETER: You think I'm talking about this hostel? Is that what you two think? I am talking about how things add up. I'm talking about what you could call—the Big Change. Do you know what I'm saying?

DIANE: Sure.

LAURA: Things have changed for you.

PETER: God damnit, not just for me!! *(Pause)* Of course nothing's really changed. It all *looks* the same—that is, physically. But everything's now so—*(Beat)* Look, who are we kidding? You two wouldn't understand. *(Beat)* You kids have any dope?

LAURA: Dope? They let you smoke in public here?

PETER: *(Smiling)* This is Europe, Miss, no one gives a fuck. If they did you think I'd be here? That's what Europe's always been—the place where no one gives a fuck—but you wouldn't remember that.

DIANE: *(Getting)* I have some grass in my room.

PETER: You do? Look, maybe later. *(Beat)* We can go outside. I know a place. I know lots of places around here.

DIANE: I thought you said no one gave a fuck.

PETER: Well, I give a fuck. I still give a fuck.

DIANE: What are you talking about?

PETER: How old are you two anyway? Nineteen? Twenty-one? Twenty?

DIANE: Yeh.

LAURA: One of those.

PETER: Figures.

LAURA: What do you mean by...?

PETER: You know how old I was when I first came here?

DIANE: No.

PETER: Do you care?

DIANE: Sure.

PETER: Then sometime I'll tell you. Remind me to open up the history books so you two can read about when I first came here. You kids can read, can't you?

LAURA: *(Smiling)* Yes, we can read.

PETER: Oh, then you must go to a private college.

(The girls laugh.)

PETER: Why is that funny? You think I'm joking? *(Beat)* You think I'm trying to be funny? *(Beat)* I insult you and you think I'm trying to make a joke? What did your shrinks tell you— everytime somebody insults you, he's really trying to be funny? Well, I'm not trying to be funny. *(Beat)* I'm trying to insult you. *(Beat)* When somebody insults you you're supposed to get pissed. Don't you learn anything anymore? *(Beat)* You know what pissed is? *(Beat)* You know

what anger is? How about mad as hell? *(Beat)* No
wonder our education system is falling apart—you
school kids aren't being taught anger anymore. *(Beat)*
In my school you could major in anger. *(Beat)* In fact,
you only had two choices for your major—anger or
premed. *(Short pause. Then they laugh; he smiles.)* How
about buying me a beer? *(They look at each other.)* Hey,
don't look at each other like I was saying fuck me,
I'm asking for a beer. What's wrong, afraid they won't
cash traveler's checks?

(Beat)

DIANE: *(Getting up)* I'll be back in a minute.

LAURA: I'll have one too, Diane.

(She goes. Pause.)

PETER: What's your name?

LAURA: Laura.

PETER: First time in Europe?

LAURA: I've been to England before—with a school
group.

PETER: Lisa's been to England with a school group.

LAURA: Laura.

PETER: Lisa, Laura, Wendy, Joanie, who the hell cares
what your name is?!! *(Beat)* I know who you are.
(Beat) Not you—but you. I was here when you
were wearing Indian print dresses. When you were
wearing T-shirts with nothing printed on them. For
eleven fucking years, I've been watching you. In your
sandals. In your Fry boots. In your Adidas sneakers.
(Beat) So what's the excuse this summer? The study of
French cathedrals or High Dutch Art?

LAURA: We're here on vacation.

PETER: In my day schoolkids didn't go on vacation,
they just dropped out for a few months.

(DIANE returns with the beers.)

PETER: Thank you. I had one of the Kennedy's kids
buy me a beer here once. You're in good company.

DIANE: It turns out that I had the grass in my purse....

PETER: Put it away.

DIANE: But you said....

PETER: I said—put it away! This isn't your country!

(Pause)

DIANE: So you come here often?

PETER: If often means every summer for the past
eleven summers, then yes, I guess you could say I
come here often.

(Pause)

LAURA: *(Standing)* Diane, I think....

PETER: Sit down! *(Beat)* I said, sit down. I want to tell
you something, I want to pass along some history to
you two kids. (LAURA *sits.*) You know what I have
seen from this table in eleven years? I have seen the
history of Western Civilization. *(Beat)* I have seen it
all. It has all passed through this hostel. *(Beat)* I was
here, ladies, when we had a reason to be here, because
we had causes then. *(Beat)* Or maybe we never had a
reason to be here, but still we had causes. Then we
didn't have causes, but at least we had tradition. Then
no more tradition even, just a history, then no more
history, only nostalgia. I've seen it all.

(Pause)

LAURA: What have you seen?

PETER: You have ten days to listen? I've seen it all and
you never will see anything. *(Beat)* In seventy-four, I
met a German terrorist here. He was taking a little R
& R. He got blown up about five months later. Maybe
it was him who got blown up, maybe he just dressed
someone like him, filled his teeth like him, and had
the joker blown up. I don't know. *(Beat)* There's a lot

of mystery in the world. a lot we can never understand.

LAURA: You met a terrorist here?

PETER: You know what that is?

LAURA: Of course I do.

PETER: Just asking. Didn't know if you kids read the paper anymore. That is if there's any paper worth reading anymore. *(Beat)* Sure you read the paper— what with the Style sections, the Leisure sections, the Food sections, you can't even call those papers anymore. Even the *Voice* and *Free Press* aren't papers anymore what with running features on finding out the best pizza joint in town. What is that? What's happened? It's hard to get a protest going against a bad pizza joint. *(The girls laugh.)* Don't laugh at that! Don't laugh at things you don't understand! Look, do you want to know what I think of you? Not just you, I mean all of you, and I've seen all of you so I know. *(Beat)* Sometimes, ladies, I get so depressed that I feel like grabbing each one of you around the neck and shaking you silly. Shaking you until you get that stupid look off your face. I just want to ask one simple question: Where the hell do you get off? Don't you understand that we did our time and it's your turn?!! *(Beat)* Don't you comprehend that? *(Beat)* Where the hell do you live? In this world or not?!

LAURA: Of course, but...

PETER: Shut up. When I say Viet Nam what comes into your mind?

DIANE: I was twelve years old when....

PETER: Shut up. Then when I say Salvador. *(Beat)* What about Salvador? There's a war. You do know that? So there's a war. So why aren't *you* out in the streets? We were. We were!!! We were in the goddamn streets. We cared. So what about you? Hav you ever even swallowed mace? What are you doing in school? What is going on in your heads? I don't understand. Who are you? Who are you? *(Beat)* Jesus, all of you make me sick. For eleven years you've made me sick. What we did, we did for you. *(Beat)* For us too. But also for you. You can't help but be sick. Please get out of my sight. *(They don't move. Long pause.)* Why are you taking this? *(Beat)* No one's ever taken this much from me before. *(Beat)* Look, why don't you just leave me alone.

DIANE: Yes, Sir.

PETER: Don't call me "Sir"! Damnit, I am thirty-three years old!

LAURA: Excuse us, Mr Thompson.

PETER: Who told you my name? *(Beat)* Hey, what is this?

LAURA: The manager of the hostel happened to tell us who you were.

PETER: Who ?

LAURA: The manager of the...

PETER: Not him. Me. *(Beat)* Who did he tell you I was?

(Awkward pause)

DIANE: You see, Laura and I are both going to law school in September.

LAURA: Diane's going to Columbia, and I'm going to N.Y.U.

PETER: Jesus Christ.

DIANE: And when the manager happened to say that you were a partner in one of the better Wall Street firms....

PETER: Get out...

LAURA: You know how hard it is for a first-year student to get a part-time job....

DIANE: ...in one of the better Wall Street firms...

PETER: Please, get out.

DIANE: We were wondering....

LAURA: We have our résumés.

PETER: Get out!!!!!

BLACKOUT

5.

Projection:

1980
THE ENVIRONMENT

(An Office. Desk. Chairs. Phone.)

(JUNE HAYES, early thirties, behind the desk. APRIL, twenties, in the chair.)

JUNE: *(Looking through a file)* I see your organization is non-profit. That helps. That certainly does help.

(Short pause)

APRIL: Why does that help, Ms Hayes?

JUNE: Because of the discount. I'll be able to offer a discount, April. Well, it's not exactly a "discount", but that's what it boils down to...for you. *(Looking through the file)* I see, twenty-one thousand members....

APRIL: What sort of discount are we talking about?

JUNE: Shall we say ten percent? Our normal commission is sixty, so let's say we'll knock off ten from that, make it an even fifty percent. April, you've picked the right time of the year to be non-profit.

APRIL: Right time? We've always been non-profit.

JUNE: The right time for *us*, dear. But I'm sure I don't have to tell you about that.

APRIL: Why don't you tell me about it?

JUNE: It's December, April. It's the end of the year. It's closing-the-books time. Taxes, April. Taxes. And I don't think it's boasting to say this year has been quite good to Stone's Phone Solicitations. Very good. You've come at the right time, just when a deduction wouldn't hurt.

APRIL: A deduction?

JUNE: So it's settled, we'll take a fifty percent commission, with of course the understanding that we are in fact taking our normal sixty, only giving ten percent back, as our way of contributing to the serious and deeply important work your organization has been doing. *(Beat)* I'll need your non-profit tax number, if you don't mind.

APRIL: Fifty percent?

JUNE: Of course we'll expect to be listed among your patrons or whatever you call your large donors....

APRIL: Excuse me, Ms Hayes—fifty percent of what?

JUNE: Of what? Of all the contributions our service solicits for you, of course. Perhaps you could even give us a page in your program, that often goes with a donation of this size, doesn't it? Something with our letterhead, congratulating you on your year—you write the copy, just send it over for approval when you get the chance....

APRIL: What program, Ms Hayes?

JUNE: The program you hand out to your audience, April. What program do you think I'm talking about?

APRIL: We don't have a program. We don't have an audience.

JUNE: No audience? I'm sure you're exaggerating, but still you're in worse shape than I thought. Think of it, an opera society without an audience.

APRIL: What opera society? We're not an opera society.

JUNE: Yes, you are, April.

APRIL: No.

JUNE: No?

APRIL: We're an environmentalist group.

JUNE: An environmentalist group? Where did I get the idea you were an opera society?

APRIL: I have no idea.

JUNE: You are sure you—?

APRIL: No opera, Ms Hayes. Clean air, clean water, endangered species, but no opera.

JUNE: Huh. *(Beat)* It must have been your logo that confused me, this big cloud blowing air. *(Beat)*

APRIL: I hope your operators will be informed about our organization before they begin their calls.

JUNE: Informed? In this case, April, I shall even do the informing myself. Which is not always the way; all of our clients are not so fortunate. *(Beat)* An environmentalist group?

APRIL: That is correct.

JUNE: I'll have to be very clear about that with our operators.

APRIL: I'd hope you—

JUNE: *(Snaps her fingers)* April, what do you think when I say—"women"? Quick!

APRIL: I don't—

JUNE: You think—mothers. You think—motherhood. You think—mother nature. And what's closer to the environment than mother nature? You following me?

APRIL: No, I—

JUNE: We use only women operators for this campaign. I mean if you'd just been a rinky-dink opera society men would have been fine, but for the environment, it's obvious it's got to be just women, don't you agree?

APRIL: I don't know.

JUNE: The female voice. Don't ever underestimate the sex appeal of the female voice.

APRIL: I won't. But getting back for a second to the fifty percent. That sounds a little steep to me.

JUNE: You've never used a professional telephone solicitation company before, have you?

APRIL: We've always tried to call ourselves. We've had volunteers.

JUNE: Volunteers are nice. They're sweet. In fact you have to ask yourself where would this country be without volunteers? I'll tell you where—it'd be bored. *(She laughs. Suddenly serious:)* April, there is a time and place for the professional. Let me show you. How much did you solicit last year? I have it right here: eleven thousand, nine hundred and twelve dollars. I can guarantee, April, that after one day of our phoning, that figure will be tripled. And tripled comes to... $33,760. Take away our fifty percent, and you have $17,880. Now you see what I mean.

APRIL: *(Beat)* You can triple our pledges?

JUNE: Mr Stone only allows us to guarantee a tripling, but generally the jump is a great deal more.

APRIL: Still, fifty percent. I don't know what our membership would think if they knew that one-half of their pledges weren't going to us. We're a very grassroots organization, our members are very committed to what we do.

JUNE: Commitment is always a good place to begin, but in this day and age, we'll have to set our sights a bit higher than just commitment. *(Beat)* If there is anything we have learned in the last fifteen years it is that. Let me show you what we can do. *(Takes out a*

large computer print-out book from her desk) Do you
know what this is? The names and phone numbers
of everyone within a three-state radius who has an
American Express card.

APRIL: I doubt if too many of our members have
American Express Cards.

JUNE: That is what we're about to change—don't
worry.

APRIL: But...

JUNE: Let me finish. I want you to know just how
much we can do for you. First we'll pick a Sunday
night to call. Why a Sunday you ask? *(Beat)* Because
that's when *Masterpiece Theater* is on, so the chances
are the right people will be home. Let's say, the third
Sunday of the month, that's before the callees have
received their bills from American Express, so they'll
feel a little more free with their expressions of
support. And that goes double if you let them charge
their pledges to their American Express Cards—so
you lose a few percent, but believe me you more than
make it up in the long run. Of course, if we're getting
heavy into plastic, I advise we look into the Diner's
Club as well—you'd be very surprised how many
people don't have both, I never could figure that one
out, one could write a dissertation on just that
conundrum, April. I'd avoid Mastercharge, I mean
Mastercard—why the hell did they change the name,
as if life weren't complicated enough already; in any
case, I'd avoid it—too many women, and they're
always saying they have to talk to their husbands
who by and large already have either Diner's or
American Express, so what's the point really, you're
just duplicating. You follow me?

APRIL: I...

JUNE: What we need is men. *Our* women talking to
those men. That's the real selling point, you see.

Young women callers with sweet *natural* voices.
Girls these men can picture wearing khaki hiking
shorts and knee socks. That's the image we have to
work to get across. *(Beat)* Now —have we discussed
the red book?

APRIL: What red—?

JUNE: We keep that in the safe, otherwise I'd show
you.

APRIL: What's to—?

JUNE: It lists those who are paying off their credit card
charges in installments. And those people, believe it
or not, are the ones most likely to give. It's true. *(Beat)*
They live life on the edge, month to month, paycheck
to paycheck; they're loose, they're free, and besides,
in this case, it's a good bet that in the last six or seven
months they've had to *use* the environment as they
usually are without enough cash in their pockets to
even go out to a movie. And you don't need cash to
take a walk in the woods, just the right clothes—and
that's what they've got their American Express cards
for. Of course, these kinds of people usually like to *get*
something for their money, that's why I'm suggesting
you seriously think about a magazine. *(Beat)* There are
plenty of nature pictures floating around you could
pick up for a song—even for no song, especially if the
magazine is getting into the right homes because
these photographers know with the right exposure
they just might pick up a little work with an ad
agency or two. *(Beat)* While we're on the subject of
gifts, you'll need something for your large donors,
the fifty-dollar people; say a birdbook, a birdfeeder,
maybe a tote bag with a bird on it; I wouldn't use
your logo on it, it would look too much like an opera
tote bag. *(Beat)* Maybe a record of wind and waves for
the twenty-five dollar givers; wind and waves are
royalty free, so it won't cost you much. *(Beat)* But

what we really need to bang our heads about is what to give the really big guns, the thousand-dollar-and-up people. I would have suggested a safari, but these money people don't have the time for that sort of thing, you have to get into their heads and figure out what they really want. *(Beat)* What do they want? *(Beat)* I'll tell you. They want to meet people, people like themselves with money and position; they want to make contacts, you give them that and they'll bite, April. *(Beat)* What about a big dinner and a show, a couple of orchestra tickets to a Broadway hit, like *Cats*, that's it, *Cats*—cats are animals, that's nature, and afterwards a party so they can mingle —I'll bet a group like yours has got a lot of pull with some of those old folk singers from the sixties; we can call it a sixties nostalgia party—what we have to keep reminding ourselves, April, is that a lot of these big executives were kids themselves in the sixties, it's *their* music—hard to fathom, isn't it, but it's true and we just have to face it. *(Beat)* Now to get the ball rolling, we can get a few stars, that's never as hard as it sounds, get them to give a little of their money—it's tax time for them too— or give a little of their time, or just their name, or even just an old necktie to auction off, whatever, just depends how aggressive we want to be. On second thought forget the necktie, what the hell does a necktie have to do with nature? Walking shoes, walking sticks, walking anything would be more like it, but who the hell walks in Hollywood, I don't know.

APRIL: *(Standing up)* Excuse me, I have to—

JUNE: One second, I want to write down Perrier for the party —that's clean water.

APRIL: I'll talk all this over with my committee.

JUNE: Picture this: We kick the whole thing off with a protest. Talk about nostalgic!

APRIL: Ms Hayes—

JUNE: We ask people to strike a match and burn a bill, say, an electric, or their oil bill, any damn bill—I'll tell you, I wouldn't mind burning my phone bill, but that's my own fault for going with a guy who's bi-coastal. But I'm not alone. There are a lot of people just like me.

APRIL: I'm sure. Thank you. *(She is trying to leave.)*

JUNE: *(Calling)* If they want to they can burn the stub they don't have to send back, what the hell, you have to start somewhere. *(Calls)* April!

APRIL: What?

JUNE: It'll be just like old times.

APRIL: Like?

JUNE: It'll feel so good to be back in a movement again.

BLACKOUT

6.

Projection:

1981
THE FREEZE MOVEMENT

(A restaurant. Table and chairs. BARBARA sits, looking over the menu.)

(Pause)

(JACK enters. Both in their thirties.)

JACK: *(Sitting)* Maria got him asleep. She's watching television now. *(He takes a drink of wine.)* Once again— thank God for the illegal alien.

BARBARA: Jack, don't say that. Don't even kid about that.

JACK: Come on, it's not exactly like we take advantage of her. She loves us. *(Beat)* Sammy loves her. *(Beat)* She's certainly a hell of a lot better off than if she were in Mexico. *(Beat)* For one she wouldn't have cable. *(He laughs.* BARBARA *laughs.)* Did you order yet? *(She shakes her head.)* I just think it is great that we can help her. *(He begins to pour more wine.)*

BARBARA: One glass. I've told you that's it while I'm nursing.

(Beat)

JACK: More for me.

BARBARA: That's why I said we should get a half of a carafe.

(He shrugs. Pause.)

JACK: How long does one nurse anyway?

BARBARA: Don't worry, I'm not going to embarrass you. *(Pause)*

JACK: Is this the place where I like the clams or the place where I don't? *(*BARBARA *shrugs. Without looking up from the menu:)* Fred's daughter's in day care already.

BARBARA: You're kidding. She can't be....

JACK: She's eleven months.

BARBARA: No she's not. She's not eleven months. I wasn't even pregnant when—what's the baby's name again?

JACK: I forget. Tamara, I think. Something like Tamara.

BARBARA: Tamara? No. George and Susan's baby is Tamara.

JACK: Maybe they're both Tamara. Maybe it's a popular name. Who knows?

BARBARA: It is not a popular name. Believe me, I am well aware of popular names. Which is why we chose "Sam". Sam isn't a popular name at all.

JACK: In any case the kid is going to day care and I'm sure Fred said she was eleven months old.

(Beat)

BARBARA: Then maybe she's a genius.

JACK: Don't be silly. *(Beat)* Fred's not a genius.

BARBARA: I wasn't serious, Jack.

(Beat)

JACK: How would you tell if your kid was a genius? Do you know? *(Beat)* Really.

BARBARA: Jack...

JACK: I'm not trying to push him, I would just like to know. Maybe there's a book we could buy. *(Beat)* What if he is gifted in something, wouldn't you like to know? *(Beat)* If we knew there could be things we could do for him, that's all. (BARBARA *laughs.*) Why is that funny? I don't understand why that is so funny?

BARBARA: Sammy is five months old, Jack. He can't even sit up.

JACK: Oh. *(Beat)* Is that bad? When do other kids sit up? *(She turns away.)* Barbara, when do other kids sit up?

BARBARA: Maybe six months.

JACK: Then I don't see why Sammy can't sit up now. Maybe if you practiced with him. *(Pause)* I'm sure he's pretty damn smart. I'm no genius, but I'm pretty damn smart.

BARBARA: What are you going to have? The clams? *(Beat)*

JACK: When I die—he will be me.

BARBARA: Jack, let's order please. *(Pause)*

JACK: You can start a kid swimming when he's Sammy's age. There are classes.

BARBARA: I know that.

JACK: We could do that. Do you know if Fred and Julie do that?

BARBARA: I don't know.

(Pause)

JACK: Oh, I wanted to show you this. *(Pulls back his jacket)* It's a button. You probably have never seen me wear a button before. We haven't known each other as long as sometimes we think. *(She looks at the button.)* It's for the Freeze Movement. *(Beat)* One of the older guys in the office had them. There was a bowl of them on his secretary's desk. *(Beat)* Didn't have to make a donation or anything. Just take one. *(Beat)* See what happens when you have a kid? You start thinking about all kinds of things again. Important things. *(Laughs to himself.* BARBARA *just nods.)* Figure I'd wear it for a while. You know. Figure it's the least I could do for Sammy. *(Beat)* The least.

BLACKOUT

7.

Projection:

1982
CIVIL RIGHTS

(A train seat. GEORGE, *mid-thirties, sits facing the audience. He talks to his young son, who is sitting in front of him, unseen. On the seat next to* GEORGE *is a large F.A.O. Schwartz shopping bag.)*

(Pause)

GEORGE: I didn't think it would be this crowded. *(Beat)* Who takes the 4:12? How can so many people afford to take the 4:12? *(Beat)* I never thought so many people took the 4:12. *(Beat)* Even on a Friday. *(Beat)* Leave your coat there on that seat. *(Beat)* If someone

wants to sit,they'll ask you to move it. *(Beat)* Don't
make it easy for them. *(Beat)* Make them ask. *(Beat)*
I don't think I'll know anyone on the 4:12. I know just
about everyone on the 5:35. *(Pause)* This is going to
be a lot of fun, Billy. I have the whole weekend
planned. *(Laughs)* I'm not going to tell you yet. I'll tell
you later. As we do things. *(Beat)* The woman I'm
seeing has an indoor pool. That much I can say. *(Beat)*
She's not rich, but she has an indoor pool. She lives in
Larchmont. *(Beat)* Her apartment building has an
indoor pool. *(Suddenly turns his head)* We're moving.
Our extra seats should be safe now. This train doesn't
stop at 125th; so we're safe. *(Looks down the corridor)*
No one's coming. *(Beat)* We're safe. *(Suddenly stands
and looks)* Everyone has a seat. We're safe. *(Beat. Picks
up the shopping bag.)* I could put this overhead if you
want. *(Shrugs and puts it back down)* I'm surprised you
didn't take the calculator. You knew you could have
had that, didn't you? *(Shrugs)* Whatever. It's your
present. Whatever you want. On these weekends,
Billy, it is whatever you want. *(Beat)* You are a
beautiful boy. *(Beat)* You look like your grandfather.
Your mother's father. Your grandfather. *(Beat)* We'll
be out of this tunnel in about ten minutes. You know,
they're fixing it up. They are finally fixing it up. The
tunnel. I heard that. *(Beat. Looks out the 'window'.)* It
doesn't look like they're fixing it up. *(Pause)* Bill. Give
Dad a hug. *(He reaches toward the audience, toward 'Bill'.)*

(Blackout)

(Immediately the lights come back up on GEORGE *sitting
back in his seat. He is looking out the 'window'.)*

GEORGE: Your mother used to work in Harlem, did
you know that? *(Beat)* Years and years and years ago.
(Beat) She used to teach. It was part of her college
program. She used to teach a couple of afternoons a
week in Harlem. *(Beat)* She loved it. She loved that
sort of thing. That was something about her that I

loved. *(Beat)* She worked out of some black church in Harlem. *(Beat)* God knows where. When you think about it now, you can just shake your head. I don't know how we did it. *(Laughs to himself)* I came that close myself to working in Harlem. They were going to build houses. Gut houses and build them. Two fellas who wanted to be ministers were doing that. I almost spent a summer with them. *(Beat)* I almost spent a whole summer building houses in Harlem. Amazing. *(Smiles)* Your mother was back in Massachusetts that summer. *(Beat)* Sh-sh. *(Beat; quietly)* I didn't realize there was a black man sitting right behind you. You always feel funny talking about Harlem around any black people. *(Long pause)* We're going to cut a tree; none of this precut stuff. I know a place. *(Beat)* I even bought an ax. Do you have snow boots? It'd be nice if it snowed. *(Beat)* Maybe next Christmas, you can spend with me. But I have you for the tree cutting. *(Beat)* That's nice for me. *(Pause)* You know, we still like each other very much. I certainly like her. So you're lucky actually. That is not always the case. It's not every divorced parents who are quite so civil with each other. *(Beat)* We respect each other very very much. You're lucky. We know that we both have rights. *(Pause)* Feel that. I love that feeling of going over the Harlem River. We'll be in White Plains in about forty minutes. *(Pause)* I can't keep my arms away from you. You do look like her. Give me another hug, Son. *(He goes to hug.)*

BLACKOUT

INTERMISSION

8.

Projection:

1983
BUYING A HOUSE

(Cafeteria in a department store. Table, two chairs. Trays of food on the table.)

(PHYLLIS and MARY, both in their thirties, are finishing lunch.)

MARY: Why am I so desperate?

PHYLLIS: You don't seem that desperate to me.

MARY: I don't?

PHYLLIS: Not to me.

MARY: Oh. Well, then, how do I seem? *(Beat)* If you don't mind my asking.

PHYLLIS: I don't mind. *(Looks at her)* Actually I'd have to say you seem relatively content.

MARY: Content.

PHYLLIS: Yes. Content.

MARY: Huh. Maybe I am then. *(Eats)*

PHYLLIS: You don't know yourself?

MARY: Who does, Phyllis?

PHYLLIS: I mean, you don't know yourself how you feel?

MARY: If I did I wouldn't be so desperate would I? (PHYLLIS *laughs. Then* MARY *laughs.*) Some days that's exactly how I seem to me too. Content, I mean. You know, when I get the odd minute to look at myself and see how I'm actually feeling. About things. About a lot of things, Phyllis. When the dust settles for a second and I can take stock of things. Sometimes I do feel very very content.

PHYLLIS: That's good to hear.

MARY: Is it?

PHYLLIS: Sure, Mary.

(Pause)

MARY: John never feels that way, I can assure you of that.

PHYLLIS: He doesn't think you're content?

MARY: I mean, about himself. Believe me, he is very very lost these days.

PHYLLIS: John? But I thought he was doing so well.

MARY: Oh sure. But that usually makes things worse, doesn't it? You know what he said to me the other day? He said "You women have it easy. You think you have it hard—but oh come on."

PHYLLIS: He said—"Oh come on"? (MARY *nods.*) What does he mean by that?

MARY: You know John.

PHYLLIS: Not really. Not since college, Mary.

MARY: He means that for a woman you can still feel good about yourself *and* go out into the business world and kick ass. In fact, we're made to feel good if we do. You know—*Working Woman* magazine and all that.

PHYLLIS: Yeh. So?

MARY: So he can't. He still has these ideas about business. I don't mean he doesn't go out and do the best he can, and he's done very well with the brokerage.

PHYLLIS: You've told me.

MARY: He is very highly respected. For his honesty. He doesn't go in for bending rules. Even if he could make a nice little profit. He's good that way.

PHYLLIS: He's always had his convictions.

MARY: Yes. Yes! He has. But still it doesn't make him feel *good* about himself.

PHYLLIS: I hope you set him straight. About what he said about women, I mean.

MARY: Sure. But you know John—really he hasn't changed that much since college. So you know him.

PHYLLIS: Then I guess I do. But he could be set straight back in college.

MARY: No, he couldn't.

PHYLLIS: I thought he could.

MARY: Trust me. I've lived with him for nine years, so I know.

PHYLLIS: I guess you would. *(Short pause)* So he thinks you have it easy with your job?

MARY: Oh no. I bring the office home with me. So he knows. He certainly knows what I go through.

PHYLLIS: Well that's good.

MARY: It's not all cherries and whipped cream in publishing, Phyllis.

PHYLLIS: I wouldn't think it would be. So who has it easy then?

MARY: What?

PHYLLIS: John saying we women have it easy.

MARY: Oh. *(Short pause)* You know.

PHYLLIS: I don't think I do.

MARY: Well—I'll bet that if one really pushed him on it, he'd say someone like you has it easy. But I know damn well you don't.

PHYLLIS: He thinks that?

MARY: Probably.

PHYLLIS: What does he think—I slept my way to where I am?

MARY: No. He's not a Neanderthal, Phyllis. He'd mean that you have been encouraged. That's all. And he hasn't. Not by anyone in particular. Not by a whole movement and so forth and so on. I mean, he'd say that you don't have to face your own beliefs every morning in the mirror. So—you can feel good about yourself.

PHYLLIS: Ah. *(Beat)* I can feel good about what I do?

MARY: Yes.

PHYLLIS: And he can't?

MARY: He might say that, yes.

PHYLLIS: Men. Jim probably thinks the same thing too. Ignorant pricks.

MARY: Yeh. *(Beat)* Yeh. *(Beat)* So now you see why I feel so desperate. About the house, I mean. I just don't know.

PHYLLIS: I don't think I can tell you what to do about the house, Mary.

MARY: Then you're neutral?

PHYLLIS: It's not something to be neutral about, is it?

MARY: Well, if you're neutral then that's as good as being for it, because I think what's bothering us the most is being criticized. You can understand that, can't you?

PHYLLIS: You have to live your own lives, Mary.

MARY: I know that. We know that. Still—it's such a *change*. John a *commuter!* That's hard to visualize for me.

PHYLLIS: We all change.

MARY: John sitting in those *commuter* trains with all the other *commuters!*

PHYLLIS: I doubt if it would be so difficult. He doesn't still always wear those black sneakers, does he?

MARY: Black sneakers?

PHYLLIS: Like in college.

MARY: Oh. No. Not for years. Not since.... *(Beat)* Styles change. *(Beat)* But still... The suburbs. A lawn. He'd look like my father when he mowed the grass. I don't know, Phyllis. It seems like quite a statement, doesn't it?

PHYLLIS: A statement to whom?

MARY: John doesn't know. Just what are we supposed to be doing? It's hard to know anymore. I don't know.

PHYLLIS: Yes.

(Long pause)

MARY: I'm having an affair, Phyllis.

PHYLLIS: Ah.

MARY: First time I've reread all those 19th century novels.

PHYLLIS: Because you are having an affair?

MARY: Once an English major always an English major. *(Beat)* Everything had become so much like work. Like maintenance. Justin. John. The office. What was I supposed to do? I didn't know.

PHYLLIS: I understand. I don't have a Justin but can understand.

MARY: I needed to. For me.

PHYLLIS: Sure.

MARY: Never before. First time.

PHYLLIS: Uh-huh.

MARY: What do you think of me?

PHYLLIS: It's your life.

MARY: Oh. You're not critical?

PHYLLIS: We do what we do.

(Pause)

MARY: Nothing shocks you, does it? Not in college either.

PHYLLIS: I wouldn't say that.

MARY: I would. Everyone did. Bet you're the same at your firm. Never-shock-Phyllis. Never could.

PHYLLIS: Well...

(Pause)

MARY: He's married.

PHYLLIS: Oh.

(Pause)

MARY: The other night after finishing one of those 19th century novels, I got this idea into my head. You want to hear it?

PHYLLIS: Sure, Mary.

MARY: I got it into my head to take his wife out to lunch and tell her. *(Long pause)* But I couldn't.

PHYLLIS: Oh.

(Silence)

MARY: I just couldn't.

(Pause)

PHYLLIS: *(Without looking at her)* So you called me instead?

MARY: Uh. That's right.

PHYLLIS: Oh.

MARY: My whole life had become like a job. Like one big business meeting. You understand, don't you? *(PHYLLIS doesn't move.)* Let me show you something. *(She takes a clipping out of her purse.)* I read this in an interview—tell me what you think. *(Reads)* "If you don't have a war going on, if you don't have a major depression, if you don't have mass starvation or various other disasters, then what you have is your personal life." *(Puts it away)* Do you believe that? *(Pause)* I don't. It's pathetic, isn't it? We're living in a whole new age today, aren't we? Where people can think such things. Aren't we? *(Pause. Picking up the check:)* Let me pay this.

PHYLLIS: No; please.

MARY: Really. *(Beat)* I insist. *(Beat)* I can write it off as a business lunch. *(She opens her purse.)*

PHYLLIS: *(Without looking at her)* Oh. Yes. Right.

(After a moment)

BLACKOUT

9.

Projection:

1984
THE LAST CIGARETTE or
THEY HAVE PROBLEMS IN CENTRAL AMERICA

(An apartment. Couch. Chair. Coffee table.)

(GEORGE, PETE, and CHERYL, all in mid-thirties. GEORGE has a pack of cigarettes, and is taking three cigarettes out.)

GEORGE: *(To CHERYL)* One for you. *(To PETE)* One for you. *(Beat)* One for me. *(Puts each cigarette on the table in front of each person)*

CHERYL: Well. Should we...?

PETE: I think, maybe....

CHERYL: Right. How about a beer?

(She is up.)

PETE: A light?

CHERYL: Sure.

GEORGE: The same.

(She starts to leave, stops.)

CHERYL: I wonder if this will take some intensity out of our lives.

PETE: Intensity?

CHERYL: You know—smoking—intense. *(Mimes smoking fast)*

GEORGE: Why would it do that?

CHERYL: I don't know. People who never smoked often seem so laid back.

PETE: That's because they think they're going to live longer.

CHERYL: Oh right. *(Starts to go. Beat)* Right. *(She goes. Pause.)*

PETE: Mint?

(GEORGE nods. Pause. GEORGE reaches into his pocket.)

GEORGE: Gum?

PETE: Spearmint?

GEORGE: Original flavor. Whatever that means.

(Takes one. Pause.)

GEORGE: Don't read the label.

(PETE looks at the label on the gum package.)

PETE: *(Reads)* "This product contains saccharin which has been determined to cause cancer in laboratory animals." *(Beat)* Gum? *(GEORGE shrugs.)* Kids chew gum. *(Shakes his head, takes out a piece)*

GEORGE: Save the wrapper.

PETE: Why? Oh. Right. Right. Can't just throw it down. Like a cigarette.

GEORGE: No.

PETE: Going to be a lot of new things like that. Now I mean. You know.

GEORGE: I know. Yeh.

PETE: I guess so.

GEORGE: Well sure.

(CHERYL *enters with the beers.*)

CHERYL: Wasn't an easy night for me. How about for you two?

GEORGE: When? Last night?

CHERYL: Yeh.

PETE: I've had easier nights. And I've had harder nights.

CHERYL: You want a glass? *(Shake their heads)* You sure? I can get you a glass, if it's what you want.

PETE: That's not what I want.

GEORGE: I know what Pete wants. Really, I think it would all be easier if we didn't talk about cigarettes for a while. Okay?

CHERYL: Okay. But before we do that, I have to tell you about last night.

PETE: Is it about cigarettes?

CHERYL: Yes. It is. *(Beat)* Last night I spent from two in the morning to four in the morning looking for a broken cigarette. I knew there was one in this apartment somewhere. I remember seeing it I think last Thanksgiving when I was cleaning up in the cabinets and in the closets before my brother and his wife and kids came for the night.

GEORGE: You mean you were going to smoke more than the five we all promised to smoke?

CHERYL: I didn't think a broken cigarette would count. Anyway it was four in the morning and you guys weren't here.

PETE: Cheryl, I'm surprised at you. Just because we weren't here? Do we have to be here?

CHERYL: Look, that's why I'm telling you, because I feel guilty, okay?

(Beat)

PETE: Then you found the broken cigarette?

CHERYL: Yeh. And I smoked it. I had to get a little piece of Scotch tape to hold it together. And then I smoked it, so shoot me. I just had to tell you. *(Pause)* I think I'll have bourbon instead of this beer. Anyone else? *(They shake their heads. She goes. Pause.)*

GEORGE: You know she should be careful using Scotch tape like that. You let it burn and you inhale that stuff you can get real sick. They ought to put a label on *that* stuff.

PETE: I know. That's why I've always used masking tape to fix a broken cigarette.

GEORGE: Yeh. Me too.

(CHERYL enters with her drink.)

CHERYL: Look, if you're trying to make me feel like shit, you've succeeded, okay? It was one lousy broken stale cigarette. It wasn't even my brand. I felt guilty the whole time I was smoking it.

PETE: No you didn't.

CHERYL: I felt guilty after.

GEORGE: Forget about it, Cheryl.

PETE: Yeh. If you want to kill yourself that's up to you.

CHERYL: It was one broken cigarette! I'm quitting, aren't I? And who are you to talk about killing yourself? You've always smoked a lot more than me.

PETE: But I have smoked low tar.

CHERYL: Since when?

PETE: Since almost always, Cheryl.

CHERYL: You call *Merits* low tar?

PETE: I do, yes, I certainly do.

CHERYL: They're no more low tar than my *Camel Lights*—?

PETE: You have got to be joking.

CHERYL: How much you want to bet?

PETE: Let me see if I understand this, you are saying that your *Camel Lights*....

GEORGE: Talk about something else, will you?

PETE: Like what?

GEORGE: I don't know.

CHERYL: Let's think of the money we'll save.

PETE: Okay. *(Beat)* Two packs a day. Three hundred fifty-two and a quarter days a year.

GEORGE: At a dollar fifteen a pack.

PETE: You pay a dollar fifteen a pack?

GEORGE: I don't buy cartons. I never could. I always felt that would make me feel like a serious smoker.

CHERYL: You are a serious smoker. You've been smoking for years and years.

GEORGE: I know. I've been a serious smoker for years.

PETE: When did you start smoking?

GEORGE: When? In college. 'Round the time of Kent State actually.

CHERYL: Huh. I thought I remembered you smoking before that.

GEORGE: No. *(Beat)* Not seriously.

PETE: I guess Kent State really affected you.

GEORGE: Oh sure. It affected you too, don't you remember?

PETE: I remember, George. But it didn't get me to start smoking seriously. I was already smoking seriously. Because I wanted to get into med school.

CHERYL: Right. I remember. I forgot you wanted to be a doctor.

GEORGE: But Kent State didn't get me started smoking. I'm not saying that. *(Beat)* I don't think it did. *(Beat)* I don't know.

CHERYL: Everyone smoked around then. During the strike.

PETE: The strike. Right. I forgot about the strike.

CHERYL: That's what Kent State means, isn't it?

PETE: Yeh, that's what it means.

GEORGE: Cheryl, some people gave up smoking during the strike, so they could donate the money they saved. My girlfriend did that. *(Beat)* She bummed from me during the strike.

PETE: Right. We all donated things, didn't we? Who were we donating things to?

CHERYL: To?

PETE: Or for?

CHERYL: I don't know. Each other I think.

PETE: Oh.

GEORGE: We used to make arm bands. And we'd smoke while we made them.

CHERYL: I even went on a hunger strike—and still I could smoke.

PETE: Yeh.

(Pause)

GEORGE: We were talking about money, weren't we?

CHERYL: Money?

GEORGE: How much money we're going to save.

CHERYL: Right. Let's see, three hundred and fifty-two and a quarter days...

PETE: Maybe I can finally pay back my college for the student loan.

CHERYL: You haven't paid that back yet?

PETE: Well, not quite. But I did give them a twenty-dollar donation last year.

GEORGE: I'd think you'd pay it off just to get them off your back. I couldn't take that shit myself.

PETE: So you paid yours off, George?

GEORGE: Not exactly. When I got out I declared personal bankruptcy. So there was nothing they could do.

CHERYL: You declared bankruptcy?

GEORGE: Yeh. *(Beat)* But I'm not suggesting Pete do that, he's got things now, I didn't have anything. So—

CHERYL: Doesn't that make you feel sort of bad, George? That was your college....

GEORGE: Well, you know, when you're a kid you do all sorts of crazy things. I figure it's all just a part of growing up.

CHERYL: Oh.

(Long pause)

CHERYL: Should we?

GEORGE: Why not?

(Each pick up their last cigarette. With a lighter)

PETE: It had to happen sometime. *(Lights* CHERYL's)

CHERYL: Thanks.

GEORGE: To think that this is it for the rest of our lives.

CHERYL: Can't we talk about something....

GEORGE: Like?

CHERYL: *(Picks up a news magazine, points to the cover)* Central America.

GEORGE: Like Central America?

CHERYL: Yeh. Like we used to.

GEORGE: We didn't sit and talk about Central America.

CHERYL: You know what I mean.

PETE: I know what you mean.

CHERYL: Thanks. *(Short pause)* They say alot's going on down there.

PETE: I know. Yeh.

CHERYL: Could be another Vietnam.

GEORGE: There will always only be one Vietnam.

CHERYL: Yeh. You're right.

PETE: Yeh. He is.

(Short pause)

CHERYL: But this Central America thing. I mean.... You know, I'll bet they don't even worry about quitting smoking down there. I'll bet they just smoke as much as they want. Both filter and nonfilter.

PETE: Yeh. But they've got a lot of other things to worry about.

CHERYL: Well we've got other things to worry about too, here, in this country.

GEORGE: Not the kinds of things that get you to stop worrying about smoking. In fact, the kinds of things we worry about only get us more worried about smoking. That's the difference between us and Central America today.

PETE: Yeh. We got our own kind of worries here.

CHERYL: At least it's good to know that if we ever decided we didn't want to quit, then there's....

(Beat)

GEORGE: There's what?

CHERYL: You know.

GEORGE: The rebels in Central America? Is that what you were going to say? That if we ever wanted to start smoking again we could just join the rebels in Central America? That is the most ludicrous thing I've ever—

CHERYL: I was joking.

GEORGE: You weren't.

(Short pause)

PETE: When did we begin to think about quitting? That's what I'd like to remember. What happened? Something must have happened?

(Short pause)

GEORGE: When I was in school, I thought I'd be dead by now.

CHERYL: Dead?

GEORGE: Like Che. Or Bobby Kennedy.

CHERYL: Oh.

(Short pause)

GEORGE: Now I don't think about being dead. I just think about dying.

BLACKOUT

10.

Projection:

1984
U.S.A.—U.S.A.—U.S.A.

(A livingroom)

(JIM in an easy chair, reading a book. LYNN enters. Both in their thirties.)

LYNN: That was Mom, she got back okay.

JIM: *(Looking at his watch)* Just now?

LYNN: Well she fed the dog first. Before calling, I mean.

JIM: Ah. *(He reads)*

LYNN: Still, must have been a lot of traffic on the parkway.

JIM: *(Without looking up)* I guess. *(Beat)* Is anything wrong?

LYNN: *(Shakes her head)* It's great to see her with Bobby, isn't it? She obviously had a wonderful time.

JIM: So did Bobby.

(She smiles and nods.)

LYNN: The phone didn't wake him, did it? *(JIM shakes his head.)* Good. *(Pause)* You checked? *(He shakes his head.)* Oh. *(Beat)* Maybe I'll....

JIM: I would have heard him, Lynn.

(She sits. Pause.)

LYNN: *(Getting up)* There's still some of Bobby's cake left.

JIM: No thanks. You have it.

LYNN: No. I'll save it.

JIM: Not for Bobby. He's had enough.

LYNN: Right. *(She sits.)* You're reading? *(He nods.)* Isn't anything on T.V.?

JIM: I didn't look.

LYNN: Oh. *(Pause)* That's a good idea. Maybe I'll read too. God I can't remember the last book I read.

JIM: What are you talking about? You're always reading.

LYNN: I haven't been always reading for—it's been years.

JIM: We have books all over this house.

LYNN: Right. The books we always used to be reading.

JIM: I really don't agree, Lynn.

LYNN: You don't? *(Beat)* So it's something we do all the time?

JIM: Not all the time. But often. Maybe not often enough. We should read more, but who couldn't say the same thing?

LYNN: Who couldn't say they should read more?

JIM: That's all I'm saying. Hell, I'll bet the head of the Library of Congress thinks he should read more and he probably does nothing but read. So just don't try to make me feel guilty. *(Beat)* If you want to feel guilty, that's your problem, just leave me out of that, thank you.

LYNN: Why would I try to make you feel guilty?

JIM: Look, if you want to watch T.V. that's fine. *(Beat)* I can go into another room.

LYNN: I didn't say I wanted to watch T.V.

JIM: Good. I think we watch too much anyway.

LYNN: That's probably true.

JIM: And so does Bobby.

LYNN: You think we let Bobby watch too much T.V.?

JIM: Yes.

(Pause)

LYNN: Is anything the matter?

JIM: No. Why does something have to be the matter?

LYNN: I didn't say something *had* to be the matter. But now I know there is, because of the way you said that.

JIM: How did I say that, Lynn.

LYNN: You know what I'm saying. Did my mother do something wrong?

(Pause. He puts his book down.)

JIM: Why don't we just watch some T.V., I can read later in bed.

LYNN: Jim. *(Pause)*

JIM: Look, it's nothing really. I don't blame your mother. She didn't mean anything. If anyone's at fault then I am.

LYNN: Fault about what?

JIM: I could have just gone with them. Then nothing would have happened.

LYNN: Gone where?

JIM: With Bobby and your mother to the dime store.

LYNN: What happened in the dime store? Mom didn't say anything happened in the dime store.

JIM: Well, nothing did happen. It's....

LYNN: What?

JIM: What she bought him, Lynn. That T-shirt.

LYNN: It's a T-shirt.

JIM: Right.

LYNN: What's wrong with a T-shirt? He picked it out himself. He loves it. He's wearing it now in bed.

JIM: I know. I looked in on him.

LYNN: I thought you said....

JIM: I looked in on him, before your mother called.

LYNN: So what is so awful about giving a five-year-old a T-shirt? At least it wasn't a gun. You know that's what he really wants, don't you?

JIM: I know he wants a gun. He's not going to get a gun.

LYNN: Mom knew that.

JIM: I know. I talked to her before they left. *(Beat)* See what I mean about him watching too much T.V.?

That's why he wants a gun. Maybe we should just put
the T.V. in the closet for a while. We could read to
him instead.

LYNN: We do read to him. But you're right, maybe we
could read more to him.

JIM: So let's put the T.V. in the closet. That's what we
said when we got married, wasn't it?

LYNN: We said we'd put the T.V. in the closet? That's
one conversation that I....

JIM: We said if we ever had a child we wouldn't let
him watch too much T.V.

LYNN: He doesn't watch that much. I know what he
watches.

JIM: I know what he watches too.

LYNN: I know you do. So what is so wrong with
giving him a T-shirt? I thought it was a good choice.

JIM: It's not the T-shirt. It's what's printed on it.

LYNN: What's printed on it? "U.S.A." is printed on it.
It just says—"U.S.A."

JIM: I know.

LYNN: So?

JIM: And that is my point, Lynn.

(Pause)

LYNN: What is your point again, I'm sorry?

JIM: *(Chants)* "U.S.A.—U.S.A.—U.S.A." Understand
now?

LYNN: Like at the Olympics.

JIM: Yeh. *(Beat)* Like at the Republican Convention.

LYNN: So?

JIM: So? It's what it means now. The militarism. The
nationalism. It was like being back in Germany in the
thirties.

LYNN: Jim, I doubt very much if our five-year-old Bobby walked into the dime store, picked that T-shirt off the counter and said to himself, "Ah, just what I want, like Germany in the thirties."

JIM: This isn't a joke.

LYNN: I'm realizing that.

JIM: They've gone and stolen the name of the country.

LYNN: Still the initials of our country, Jim, aren't exactly a swastika.

JIM: Not yet. *(Beat)* Not yet. But they're trying!

LYNN: Look, I feel the same way as you do, but we are just talking about a T-shirt.

JIM: I'm sorry, but I'm talking about a lot more than a T-shirt. Something has to be done, Lynn. I realize that now. When I walked into his room and saw my son sleeping and those letters across his chest, I realized that. That's not his country. "U.S.A." is not his country. We're his parents and we have to recognize that.

LYNN: Jim...

JIM: It suddenly dawned on me, while I was in his room, that finally I had something to fight for again. I had him. They're fighting to take him from us, Lynn. From what we believe. And we have to fight to keep him from them.

LYNN: *(Yells)* Who's them?!!!!

JIM: *(Upset)* You know! You know! *(Chants)* "U.S.A.— U.S.A.—U.S.A.!!!!" *(Beat)* Damn it, enough is enough. It's time we got off our butts and did something. Not for us anymore, Lynn, but for him. It's time we took a stand. *(Beat)* That's what I'm doing.

LYNN: Taking a stand?

JIM: That's right. *(Beat)*

LYNN: With a five-year-old's T-shirt? *(Beat)* That's your stand?

JIM: It's something. *(Beat)* Damn it, it's something. *(Beat)* Lynn, it's something. *(Pause)*

LYNN: Sure.

BLACKOUT

11.

Projection:

1986
"THE CHERRY ORCHARD"

(A room in a house that has been closed-up; a few chairs, with dustcovers. LIBBY; *her brother,* FRANK; *and his wife,* JUDITH, *sit and wait.)*

(Pause)

LIBBY: Have you been watching the Irangate hearings? *(*FRANK *shakes his head.)* Neither have I.

FRANK: What a ridiculous name.

(Short pause)

JUDITH: I watched a little. I couldn't take more. You watch and end up asking yourself— Well— *(She looks at* FRANK.*)* I don't know. *(Beat)* Why *do* we have to tear everything down? We're just not happy unless we're destroying, are we?

FRANK: No, I don't think we are. *(Beat)* Though not everyone anymore. I wouldn't include everyone. *(*JUDITH *nods. Short pause. To* LIBBY*)* By the way I brought different colored stickers. We each take a color, you, Tom, and me, and mark what furniture we each might want to keep. Then, I guess, we sort of horse trade. *(He laughs.)* There's a book about dividing things up. About estates. They have a lot of great suggestions like that. *(Short pause)* We could start—

LIBBY: Wait for Tom, he'll be off soon. *(Short pause)*

JUDITH: Odd, sitting here without your mother. She'd never have let any of you three kids sit like this here, without her being a part of it.

LIBBY: She still is a part of it. She is the reason for it.

JUDITH: Of course, I didn't mean—

FRANK: Judy meant, Libby, that Mom would have really enjoyed this. All of us together; sitting around her livingroom. *(Beat)* She missed that. She always told me on the phone how much she missed that. *(Beat)* But of course she's here in spirit. *(To* JUDITH*)* And that's all Libby meant.

(Short pause)

LIBBY: *(To* JUDITH*)* I don't think I've thanked you for your note. I was very touched.

FRANK: She writes wonderful notes, doesn't she?

LIBBY: If this was any indication—

FRANK: The one she wrote to Tom, you could publish it, I think.

JUDITH: Frank—

FRANK: I'm serious. *(Beat)* Take a compliment. Libby was complimenting you.

(Short pause)

JUDITH: I figured that since because of the kids, I couldn't come right away, with Frank, then at least—Well— *(She looks at* FRANK.*)* I wanted you to know that my thoughts were with you.

LIBBY: You made that clear, thank you.

JUDITH: I felt bad; if Pete hadn't just been getting over the—

LIBBY: Judy, please, you do not owe anyone an apology.

FRANK: That's what I told her too, Libby. Judy, come on now, just forget it. *(Beat)* We're all here now. *(Beat)* We all were at the funeral.

*(*TOM, LIBBY *and* FRANK's *younger brother, enters.)*

TOM: That was Taylor. *(Beat; he sits.)* He'll take the case. I told you Frank we'd get someone.

FRANK: And I said, I don't think we should—

TOM: Let me finish. He'll split what we win, so we pay him nothing. That *was* your concern, Frank, that we pay him nothing.

FRANK: *(To himself)* Shit.

JUDITH: *(Trying to calm him)* Frank—

FRANK: Where did he get this guy?

TOM: *You* said if we paid him nothing.

FRANK: But there is no case! I'm a doctor, Tom, there's no grounds here for malpractice. What kind of shit lawyer—

TOM: You went to high school with Taylor—

FRANK: From what I remember about the high school in this town that is not a recommendation. *(Beat. To* LIBBY:)* He's found an ambulance chaser. We're supposed to put ourselves through hell—

TOM: *(To* LIBBY*)* He's president of the Optimists Club. You've seen him. He's very well known in this town.

LIBBY: Taylor? What's his first name?

TOM: George. I think, George.

FRANK: *(To* LIBBY*)* When I said, okay as long as it doesn't cost us anything, the estate anything— I also meant the emotional cost. Do you know, Libby, what the emotional cost of something like this can be? Do you have any idea?

JUDITH: *(To* LIBBY*)* A friend of Frank's was sued for malpractice. He'd done nothing. His wife, just her, lost about forty pounds; she was down to nothing—

TOM: I don't care about the doctor, Judith!!

FRANK: *(Yells)* Don't shout!! *(Beat)* Look, if all we're going to do is shout—

TOM: Look. It's not the money. I don't care about that. We can give that away. Flush it down the toilet.

FRANK: *(To* LIBBY*)* An intelligent comment. Tom always did have a peculiar way of managing his money, didn't he?

TOM: *(To* JUDITH*)* But come on, listen to me, she goes in for a physical from this guy, he says he can find nothing wrong— This is a complete physical, or at least that's what she paid for—

JUDITH: I know all this, Tom.

TOM: *(Ignoring her)* And within four weeks, she's falling down steps, and she's got a tumor the size of a—

FRANK: That can happen!

TOM: Then we'll see in court, won't we? Taylor has no qualms about taking this all the way to—

FRANK: *(To* LIBBY*)* He's not going to get me sitting in a courtroom.

LIBBY: If you're talking to Tom, talk *to* him.

FRANK: *(To* LIBBY*)* I'm not going to listen to lawyers pick over an autopsy report of my mother!

TOM: You don't have to do shit, Frank. Fly back to Phoenix. Forget about everything. Forget about us. *(Beat)* Leave us in peace.

LIBBY: Tom—

TOM: I'll drive you to the airport. When do you want to go?! *(Beat)* Just say when.

(Short pause)

JUDITH: Our flight isn't for another four hours.

TOM: They've got a nice lounge there you could wait in. If that's what you want to do.

(Pause)

FRANK: She was my mother too, Tom, you're not the only one who's upset.

(Pause)

JUDITH: *(Getting up)* Maybe your mother left some coffee. *(Beat)* Of course there won't be any milk....
(She goes. Pause.)

FRANK: *(Gets up and walks around)* Why? Why do we always look for someone or something to blame? I guess that's just human nature, right? I do understand, Tom, I really do. *(TOM laughs.)* What? What is humorous about that? *(Pause)* The facts are: Our Mother has died. And a malpractice suit is not going to bring her back, pal. I know that. *(Beat)* Libby knows that.

LIBBY: Speak for yourself, Frank.

FRANK: So speak then. *(Short pause; he shrugs and continues.)* Such a suit, I promise you, will only cause us all considerable pain. And for what? You've said it's not the money. So it must be to get even. Is vengeance what you're after, Tom?

TOM: *(To LIBBY)* Taylor also said that since Mom smoked throughout the fifties, he'd try to get her name on a class action against the tobacco companies. *(Beat)* They say it's only time before one of those is won. The tide seems to be turning, he says.

FRANK: Fuck! *(Short pause)* Will you ever grow up, boy? *(Beat)* So it has to be multinationals that killed our mom. It's big business; so that's the murderer! Pretty soon, you're going to end up blaming President Reagan! Don't you see how pathetic you've become,

Tommy?!! *(Beat)* Get off your high horse, and you'll
see that this country is not as awful as you think.
(Beat) But then again, I don't delude myself for a
second that I can convince you of this. *(Beat)* So let's
just say we see the world a little differently.

TOM: No argument there. *(Short pause)*

FRANK: And as I said, she is my mom too. So you
can tell your shit lawyer to kiss off. *(Pause)* Hey look,
when I walked into this house, ask Judith, I must have
turned as white as a sheet. I don't want time to pass
by either. I don't want people I love to die. But they
do. It does. It has. *(Beat)* *(Laughs to himself)* Having
kids, you really get to see the time go by. I'm really
sorry you both— But there's still time. Mom loved
grandkids, you know. *(Beat)* She doted on Pete. I'd
say if we really cared about doing something for
Mom—

LIBBY: Shut up, Frank. *(Beat)* You want a family. Fine.
Fine. But just shut up.

(Long pause)

LIBBY: Hey. We have things we have to get done.
Right? Frank and Judy have a plane to catch. *(Beat)*
Here, I've written the thank-you notes; I thought it'd
be nice if we all signed; that's how Mom always made
us do it. *(Beat)* Even when she wrote our thank-you
notes herself.

TOM: *(Smiling)* So you're Mom now? *(Beat)* I wouldn't
object.

FRANK: Give me a stack, I'll sign. *(Beat)* You should be
thanked for thinking of this, Libby. Thank-you notes
never entered my mind.

LIBBY: Your wife reminded me.

(Pause as they begin to sign.)

TOM: Does it matter who signs first? Should I leave a
space?

LIBBY: No. No, it doesn't matter.

(Short pause)

FRANK: *(Looking at one card)* The O'Hara's flowers I thought were especially beautiful. Maybe I should say that.

LIBBY: I did. *(Beat)* Did you read my note? Both of you are just signing your names without reading my notes?? How do you know what the hell I've said?

FRANK: *(Trying to make a joke)* God Tommy, Mom makes us not only sign our names but we have to read what she writes, too. *(He laughs; no one else does.)*

TOM: Flowers. Mom, I'm sure, would rather have had the money go to—

FRANK: Mom loved cut flowers.

TOM: I didn't say she didn't. *(Beat)* When Dad died, we asked people to give donations to somewhere.

FRANK: That was your idea, not hers. One more thing you shoved down our throats.

TOM: Not true. You know that isn't true.

FRANK: *(Ignoring him, looking at a card)* Who's the Reverend William Hackler? He wasn't the new assistant minister I met—

TOM: He's the reverend of the Baptist Church on First Street.

FRANK: That was a black church.

TOM: It still is.

(Short pause)

LIBBY: Mom did a lot of volunteer work there these past couple of years. I just found out about it myself.

TOM: A few weeks ago Hackler shows up at the hospital— And he and Mom begin to have this conversation.... *(Beat)* She told no one what she was doing.

FRANK: *(Signs his name and goes to another card)* Mom.
Dear Mom. *(He smiles and shakes his head.)*

TOM: What does that mean? *(Beat)* What the hell does
that mean?! *(Beat)* You think it was stupid or
something for her to volunteer to work at a black—

FRANK: Get off my back!!! *(Beat)* I didn't say anything.
(Beat) Mom was a character, okay? We all knew that.
One loveable, a bit eccentric, maybe overly generous
character. *(Short pause)*

FRANK: *(To* LIBBY*)* He wants to turn me into a racist
now. *(Laughs)* Why?? Because I happen to disagree
with him on a few things. Tolerant, aren't we, Tom?
(Beat) What else are you going to beat your chest
about? Next will it be that I'm anti-Semitic because I
don't happen to pray every morning in the direction
of your *New York Times?!! (Laughs)* You should really
see the rest of this country, Tom. You should see just
what a dinosaur you have become. *(To* LIBBY*)* I have
a Chicano nurse and secretary, Libby. The son of
one I'm helping through college. The University of
Arizona. *(To* TOM*)* I try to help where I can. What the
hell do you do, besides lecture people?!! *(Beat)* You
want to know who is really closer to Mom, to the kind
of help she was trying to—

TOM: *(Yells)* You aren't!! You aren't!!!

*(*FRANK *is laughing.)*

LIBBY: Stop laughing Frank.

(Pause. They continue to sign cards.)

TOM: *(To* LIBBY*)* Tell me, am I crazy or what,
but wasn't there a time long ago when the word
"conservative" meant something—bad?

(Beat; then LIBBY *laughs and* TOM *laughs.)*

FRANK: I don't know, was it ever bad to *eat*
conservatively; *drive* conservatively; *drink*

conservatively, which, after watching you these past two days, Tom, I suggest you begin to think about. *(Short pause)*

TOM: *(To* LIBBY*)* First they appropriate the flag, now they're after "health". Incredible.

FRANK: The flag we didn't wait to appropriate, we grabbed it out of your hands to stop you from burning it.

TOM: The hypocrisy! *(Beat)* Or is it amnesia? *(To* LIBBY*)* You remember, don't you, sitting up with Mom and Dad and Frank and listening to them make plans for Frank to go to Canada?

FRANK: I didn't go, did I?

TOM: Because of the lottery. You got something like three hundred and thirty in the lottery!!!!

FRANK: You want to know what I think you people's problem is?

TOM: Who's "you people"?

FRANK: *(Ignoring him)* You have to make everything a world cause. Everyone has to join in. Everyone has to follow you. Think like you. Believe in what you believe. But things have changed, Tom. Look around. Take a trip. Come and visit us. *(Beat)* What you'll realize, I swear to you, is that you need to relax. I say this now as a brother. Look at your drinking for Christ sake.

TOM: I don't drink—

FRANK: Mom was relaxed. You want to be like her? Keep her ideals alive? Okay. But she didn't try to change the world. She didn't make a big *show* out of what she did. You just said that yourself. *(Beat)* Why does one person feel the need to impose his beliefs on another person? This is what I do not get. People are not as dumb as you people in the East think they are. *(Beat)*

FRANK: Politics. Politics. Where does that get you?
Lay off for a while; I promise you, it'll change your
life. *(Beat)* Always this attacking everything. Standing
up for what? Attack attack blame blame. Like with
Mom's death. She died for Christ sake, let her lie in
peace. Let us live in peace. *(Beat)* Just get on with life.
Move on.

TOM: Grow up?

FRANK: Your words, not mine, but I'm not arguing.
(Short pause) So—yeh, grow and begin for a change to
look at things positively. You'll be amazed what
a relief it is to stop finding fault with everything.
I promise, you'll feel good.

JUDITH: *(Entering with coffee)* Sorry I took so long with
the coffee, but—

TOM: *(To* FRANK, *interrupting)* Is that the point now,
Frank—to feel good?!

FRANK: What is wrong with that? *(Beat)* I see nothing
wrong with that.

(Short pause)

JUDITH: Uh, I did a little cleaning around the stove,
that's why— If the real estate people are coming by—

LIBBY: What real estate people?

FRANK: Just to set a price. Just so we can see what it's
worth. I figured while we're still here— I know we
haven't decided to sell. I'm not pushing anything.
I am just getting the facts. *(*JUDITH *sets down the coffee.)*
I'll get those colored stickers. They're in Tom's car.

TOM: It's open.

FRANK: *(Starts to leave, stops)* I'm glad we talked, Tom.
(Beat) It seems like years, doesn't it? Don't
misunderstand me, I know there are a lot of things
wrong with the world, but— and this is a big
"but"—things are also not as bad as you think.

TOM: Maybe not for you. *(Pause)*

FRANK: So, I am one of the fortunate ones. You think I should be sorry for that? *(He goes.)*

JUDITH: No one takes sugar, do they?

LIBBY: I do.

JUDITH: Oh. *(Beat)* I'll check in the pantry.

LIBBY: *(Without meaning it)* I can look if you—

JUDITH: No, no. Let me. It's been a hard day for all of you, I'm sure. *(She goes. Pause.)*

TOM: *(Finally)* Listen.

LIBBY: What?

TOM: Hear that?

LIBBY: What? No.

TOM: It's Mom and Dad. *(Beat)* They must have been listening. *(Beat)* Because they're crying now.

BLACKOUT

12.

Projection:

1988
THANKSGIVING

(A kitchen in a farm house in the country.)

(The table has been partially cleared. BILL, ALICE, WILLA, and FRED. They are all in their late thirties.)

(As the lights come up:)

FRED: *(Yells at WILLA)* You bitch! God damn you! So this is how you tell me?!!!

(Awkward pause)

WILLA: *(To ALICE and BILL, as she goes)* Excuse me.

(After a beat, FRED follows her out.)

(Pause)

BILL: *(Continues to clear the table)* Does it still drive you crazy when the napkins don't match?

ALICE: It's your house. *(Beat)* And it never "drove me crazy".

BILL: We fought about it once.

ALICE: I doubt if we were fighting about matching napkins, Bill. *(Nods toward where* FRED *and* WILLA *exited)* Maybe I should—

BILL: Let them talk.

ALICE: They've been talking for twenty years.

BILL: Let them be alone.

ALICE: They're our friends.

BILL: That's what I'm saying.

(Pause; they continue to clear and begin to set the table.)

ALICE: Incredible. *(He looks at her, then continues to set the table.)* You want to know what's incredible? We're here for no more than a half an hour and already....

BILL: It embarrasses you ?

ALICE: Of course not. Is that what you think? *(Beat)* It troubles me, that's all. They're my friends. (BILL *leaves.)* Where are you—?

*(*ALICE *sits. Pause.* BILL *returns with napkins.)*

BILL: I have four blue ones. Someone will have to be different. I'll be different. Where should I sit? *(Beat)* I'll take the head, it's my house after all. *(Beat)* The kids are eating in front of the T.V. I told them they could. *(Beat)* They asked. *(Beat)* I'll set up a table for them.

ALICE: They can hold their plates on their laps. My kids do it all the time.

BILL: Katie doesn't. *(Beat)* Katie doesn't watch T.V. while she's eating "all the time". Katie's your kid too.

ALICE: Yes. *(Beat)* And she's beautiful, Bill. *(Gets up and starts to set the table)* How many times do I have to say that?

BILL: I don't know.

ALICE: You've raised her beautifully.

(Short pause)

BILL: And those two little jokers of yours out playing on my lawn, they aren't so bad either.

ALICE: No? No, they aren't, are they? But obviously that's all Bob's doing. Not mine.

BILL: *(Smiles)* Obviously. *(Beat)* No other explanation.

(She smiles and nods; they continue setting the table.)

ALICE: *(Relaxed for the first time)* You know we should do this more often. Maybe next Thanksgiving when we really have a reason to celebrate.

BILL: What reason's that?

ALICE: Thanksgiving. *(Beat)* It's a holiday. We could celebrate the holiday. *(Beat)* Jesus, that's what people do, Bill. They celebrate holidays.

BILL: Getting friends together for a weekend, for me that's reason enough to—

ALICE: I didn't mean—

BILL: What did you mean? Are you saying you have to have Hallmark Cards tell you when you can celebrate—?

ALICE: Lay off me, Bill. *(Beat)* I'm not going to fall for that crap, okay? *(Beat)* You want to win an argument? Okay, I concede, you've won the argument. *(Pause)* Shit. I'm sorry.

BILL: No, you were right, Alice.

ALICE: Now you're trying to make me feel awful.

BILL: I'm trying to do nothing. *(Beat)* Which seems to be impossible.

(Short pause)

ALICE: *(Nods toward the exit)* It's them. They've—
A mood has been set, I guess.

BILL: Hey, did you see Katie's report card?

ALICE: Twice. But I'll be happy to look at it again.

BILL: Later. When everyone is back. When she's
around.

ALICE: Good idea. Some positive feedback. It'll do her
good.

BILL: She's already doing great.

ALICE: Yes, she is. She is one terrific young lady. *(Beat)*
I for one would love to have her disposition. And the
glow she has. She walks into a room— Is it youth,
Bill? Is it her? I don't think I had anything like the—
You know, when I was her age.

BILL: You're going to paint her portrait.

ALICE: She said she'd let me? She told me she'd think
about it.

BILL: Bob brought it up. The moment you guys
walked in he brought it up. As if he had to convince
me.

ALICE: It'd take about a week. She could come down
to the city and stay with us.

BILL: You could do it here.

ALICE: Sure. We could.

(Short pause)

BILL: Where's your husband with the food? The
store's only right down the road. *(Beat)* I'm glad that
you started to paint again, Alice. What a waste when
you gave it up.

ALICE: I remember you saying that at the time.

BILL: I'm glad that you remember that.

(Short pause)

ALICE: It's all come back. It's like I never stopped for a minute. In fact, I'd like to show you a few things when you have a minute. I value your opinion. You of all people would understand— *(Beat)* I have slides. The pieces are huge. *(Beat)* The slides are in the car. When Bob gets back.

BILL: Anytime. I'd love to.

ALICE: *(Laughs)* Though I have to confess that I always felt you were a little too easy on me. You always liked pretty much everything I did. So— *(Beat)* Now, I want you to be critical. Tell me what you really think. *(Beat)* I can take it now. *(Beat)* I know I'm good.

BILL: I've always known that.

ALICE: So—be critical then.

BILL: Why?

(Short pause)

ALICE: I mean I really want you to be serious. I'm taking this serious now.

BILL: I've always been serious about what you showed me.

ALICE: I want your opinion about what you think is the best.

BILL: I'm your friend not a judge, Alice. *(Beat)* Show them to me. Let me love them all. God, I know how unfashionable that is, but give that to me, okay? *(Beat)* Let me love them— uncritically.

ALICE: I'm trying to sell—

BILL: I don't care.

(Pause. BOB, late thirties, enters with a bag of groceries and a six pack of beer.)

BOB: Sorry. There was a line. You'd think you were at Zabar's for Christ sake. Who the hell lives up here?

BILL: Those were weekenders.

BOB: Of course. So it was like Zabar's. *(Starts to empty the bag)* What's the matter with Willa and Fred?

ALICE: Why? What are they doing?

BOB: Nothing. Just sitting in the backseat of Bill's car.

BILL: Talking?

BOB: They're not fucking.

BILL: Willa dropped her bomb. While Fred was washing the lettuce.

BOB: Why does that sentence not make any sense?

ALICE: She's taken a job at the University of Arizona. She didn't get tenure here.

BOB: She wasn't really expecting—

BILL: And Fred was just told. While he was washing the lettuce. She leaves in three weeks.

BOB: "Just told?" Christ. *(Beat)* Who's making the sandwiches?

ALICE: I think we're all going to help ourselves. Just leave everything out. The kids are eating in front of the T.V.

BOB: Where else do kids eat? *(Beat)* By the way they're having a great time out there. You should invite us more often. Or am I being too subtle? *(Laughs)*

BILL: No. Subtlety was never one of your big problems.

ALICE: We were just talking about Thanksgiving.

BOB: Great. The kids will love it. A real traditional celebration.

ALICE: Actually, Bill was just saying—

BILL: Forget it.

ALICE: But—

BILL: Shut up.

(Pause)

BOB: What's—? *(Short pause)*

ALICE: It's not between us, Bob. *(To BILL)* He's always worried that we're going to get into something.

BILL: We're fine.

BOB: I didn't say—

ALICE: Ex-couples *can* be good friends, Bob. Someday you will realize that.

BOB: When will that be?

ALICE: I didn't mean— Look, what you're feeling— It's in the air. You missed Fred blowing up.

BOB: I see.

BILL: We're fine.

BOB: Good. *(Short pause)* It seems like they've been together for hundreds of years.

ALICE: Fred and Willa? Not this time.

BOB: In college they were together.

ALICE: For the last three years. After the middle of sophomore year. And that lasted a couple of years after school, no more. *(Beat)* They broke up while they were in graduate school. *(Beat)* They stayed together for a while—in the same apartment—because they couldn't afford two places. *(Beat)* But by then they were just friends. *(Beat)* They each dated. You remember, Bill?

BILL: I know what Bob means, you think of them as a couple. I do.

ALICE: Ten months this time, that's all. Ask them. They've been friends but not—

BILL: During Watergate they got back together for a while. As a couple. I remember going over to Fred's apartment in Middlebury to watch the hearings. And they were definitely together at that point.

ALICE: Watergate wasn't forever.

BILL: No. *(Beat)* That lasted that time, maybe—ten months again. Maybe ten months is their limit now.

BOB: *(Laughs)* Watergate. Funny what brings people together, then what pulls them apart.

BILL: I wasn't saying Watergate brought them back together. I just meant that time. I was referring to a period—

BOB: Sure. Sure.

ALICE: So what's pulling them apart?

BOB: I don't know. She didn't get tenure.

BILL: She could have stayed on one-year contracts. I know this for a fact. From our dean.

BOB: Then—I don't know. *(Beat)* I suppose that is what they're talking about now. *(Beat)* Maybe we shouldn't wait for them before we eat. *(From outside a four-year old boy cries. BOB looks out.)* It's Jason. *(Turns to ALICE)* I'll go if you want.

ALICE: I can go.

BOB: No. No. *(He goes. Pause.)*

ALICE: *(Finally)* So—why do you think she's leaving him?

BILL: Willa? *(Short pause)* Or are we now talking about you? Why you are leaving Bob.

(She turns to him; short pause.)

ALICE: You know? It's that obvious?

BILL: No. It's not. *(Beat)* Quite the opposite. I only just realized this second. *(Beat)* You're both very calm about it.

ALICE: He doesn't know. *(Short pause)* Don't look at me like that. He'll fight for custody. I need to have my case first. I don't want to give him an advantage.

BILL: An advantage? You haven't told him you're leaving him?!

ALICE: He's a lawyer, Bill. He's going to rip me apart.
It's going to be very ugly, I'm sure. I need to be
prepared.

BILL: He's your husband.

ALICE: He'll go crazy. I don't need that right now.

BILL: Alice—

ALICE: I came to you as a friend.

BILL: And what do you want me to do?

ALICE: Don't judge me. *(Beat)* Listen to me. Talk to
me. But don't judge.

(Short pause)

BILL: Come here. *(He hugs her.)* Come here. *(Hugs her
tighter)* Roots in water.

ALICE: What?

BILL: Roots in water. We live, but there's nowhere to
settle. *(He looks at her.)* A poem. That I've been
working on for a long time.

END OF PLAY